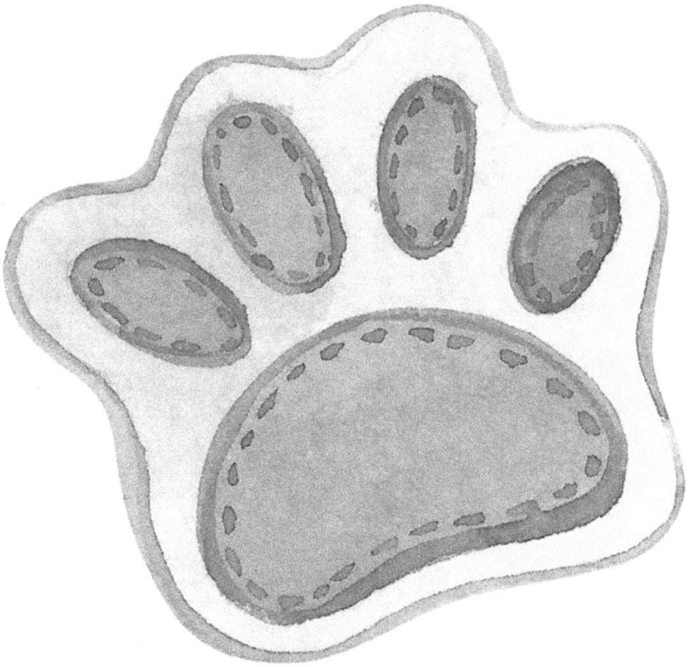

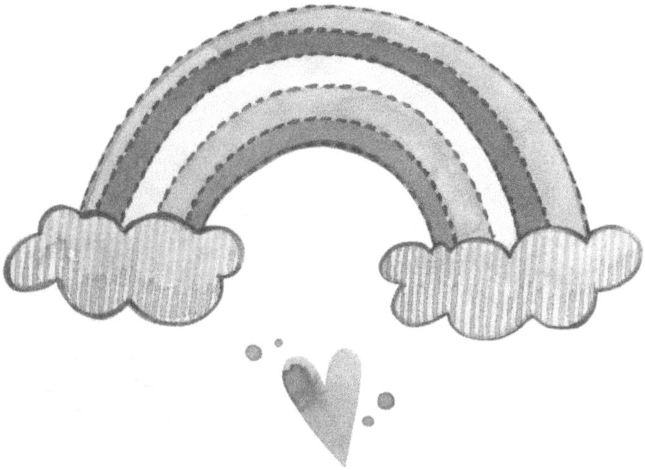

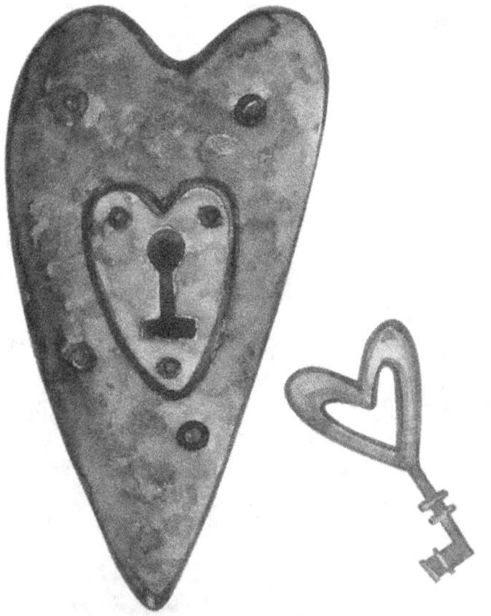

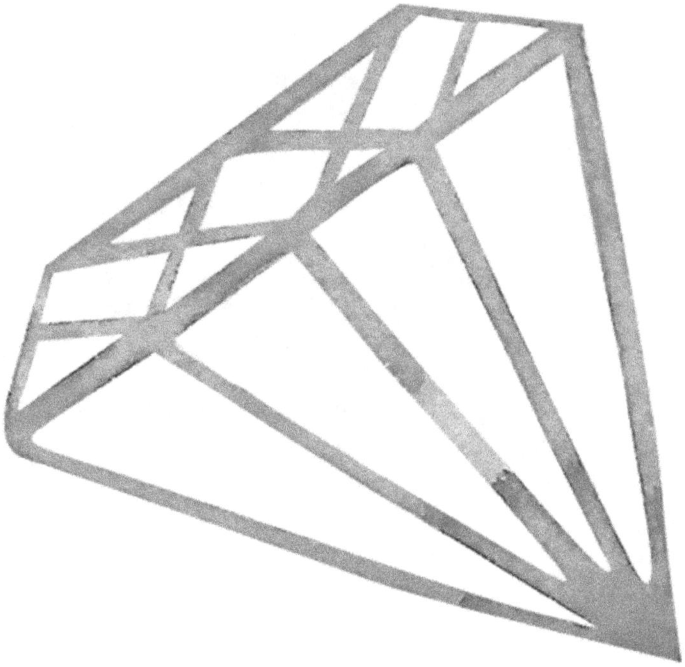

you
+
me
=
love

i love you

love you

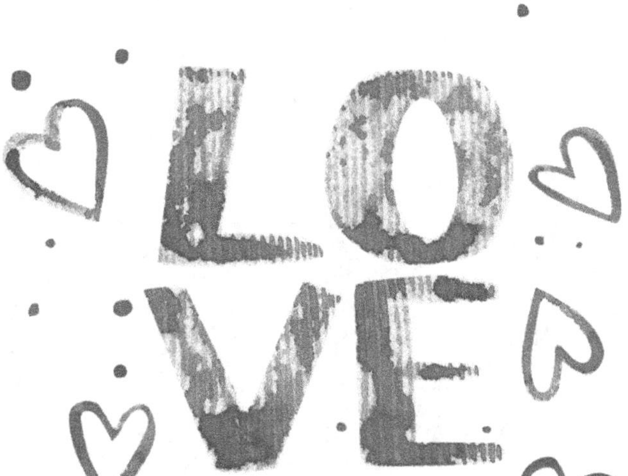
LOVE

you are loved

love is all you need

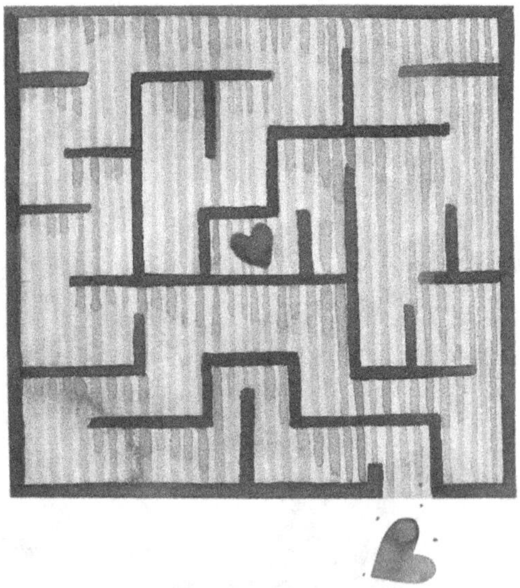

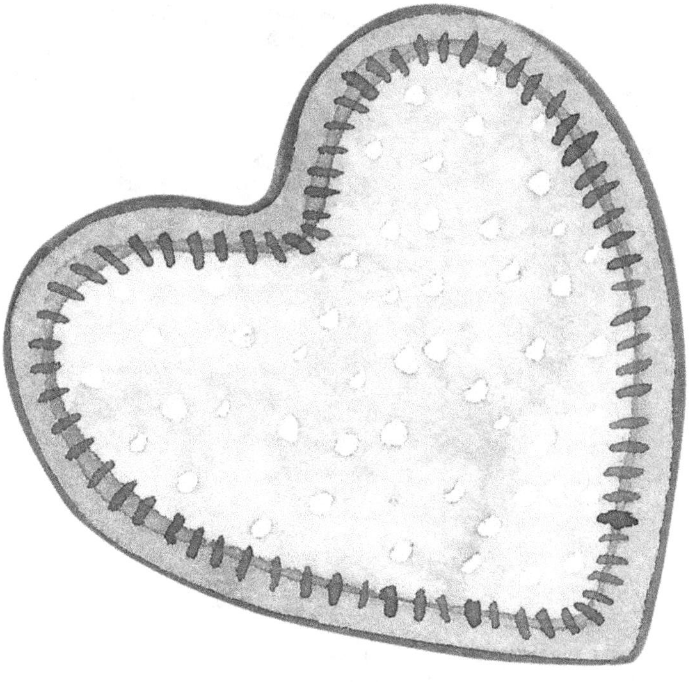

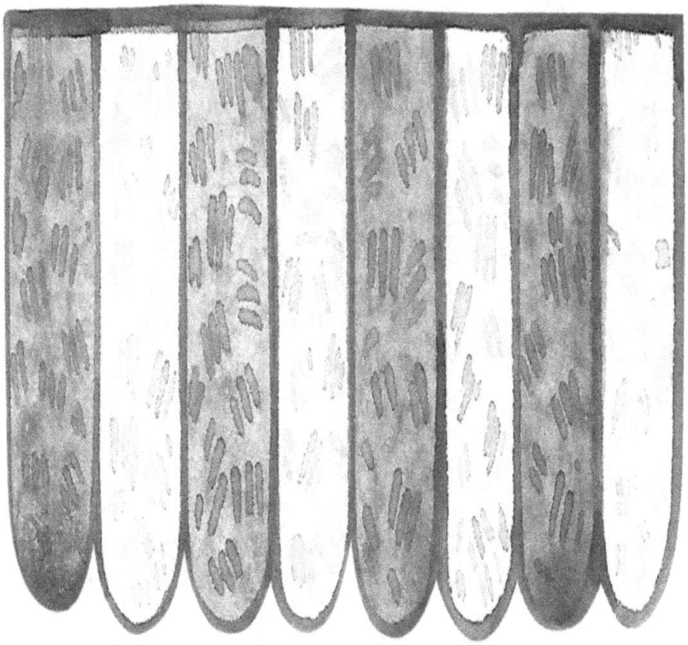

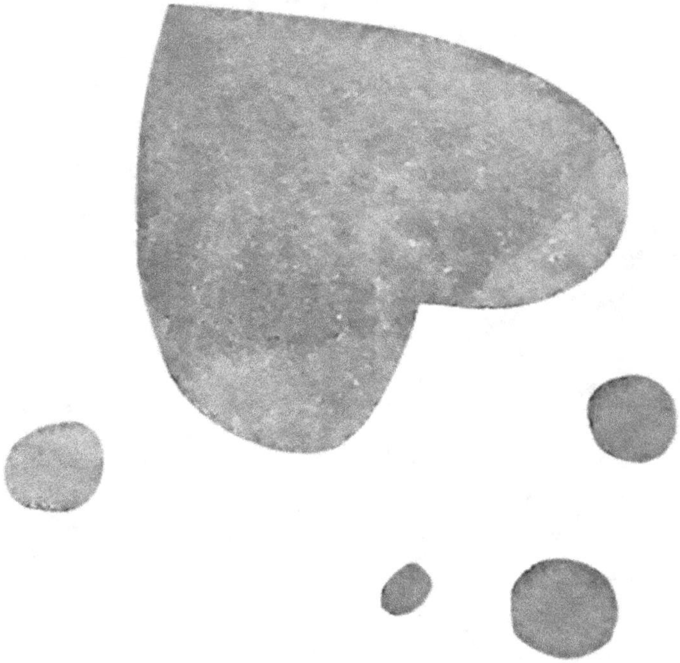

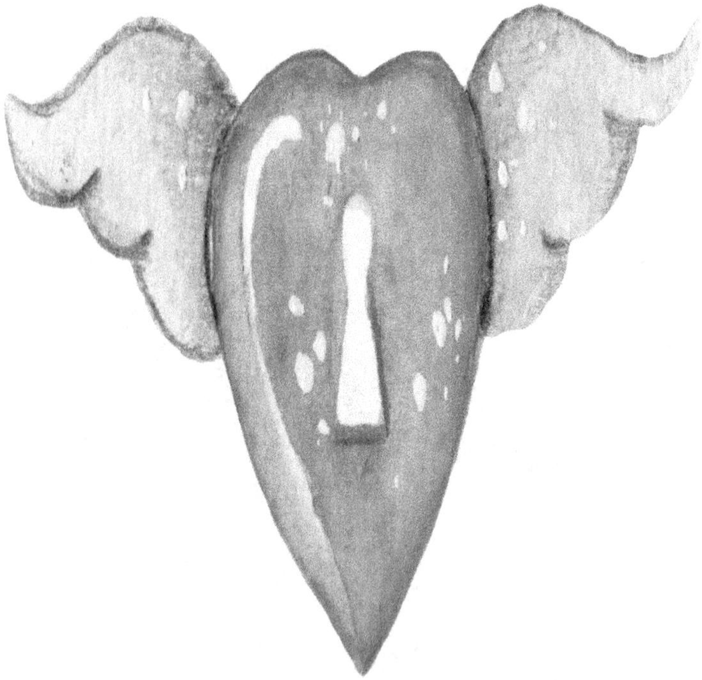

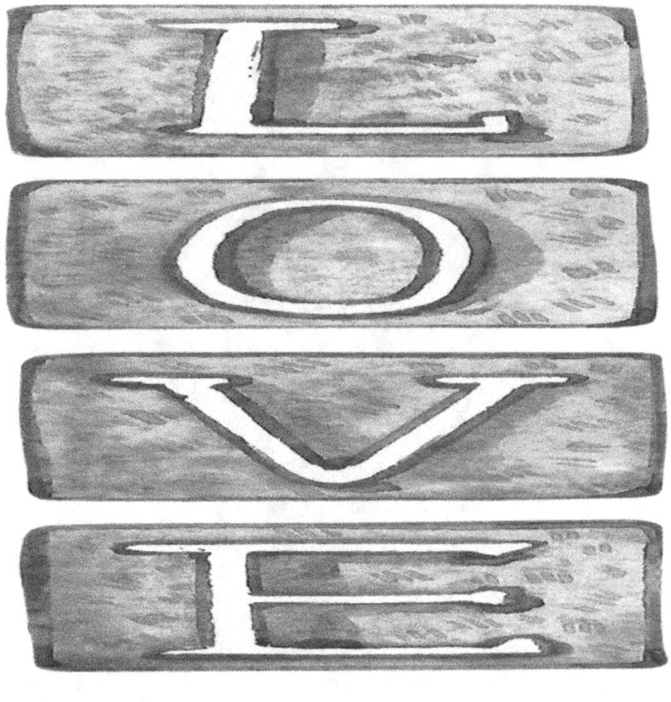
L
O
V
E

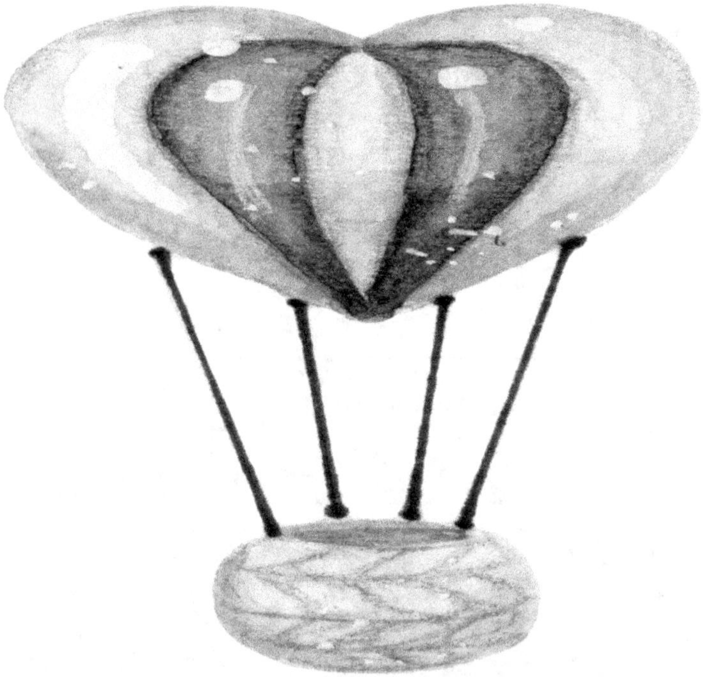

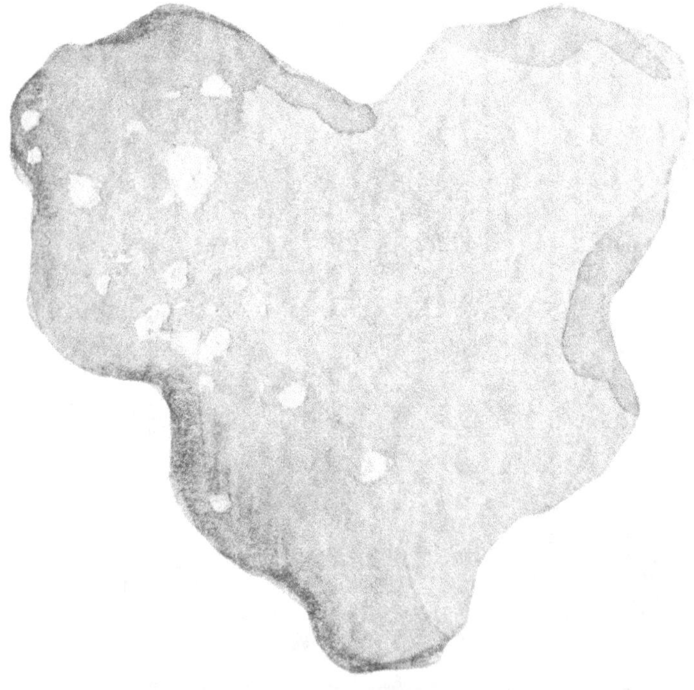

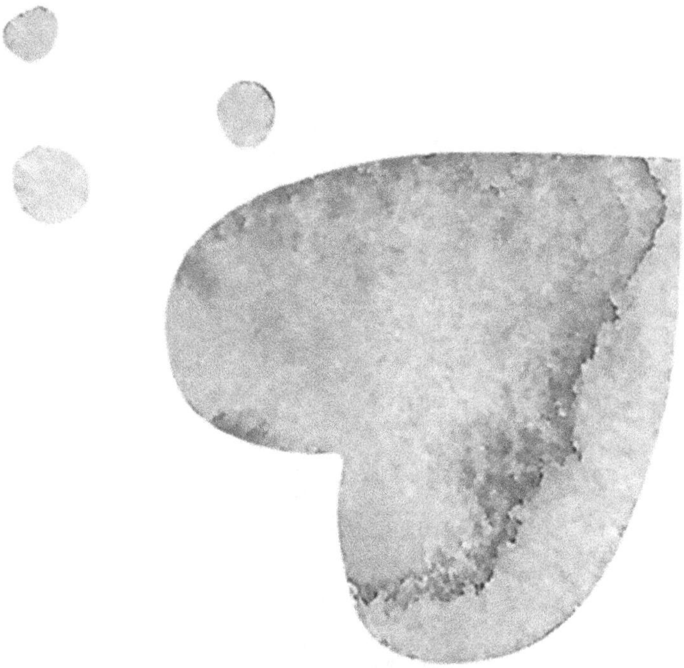

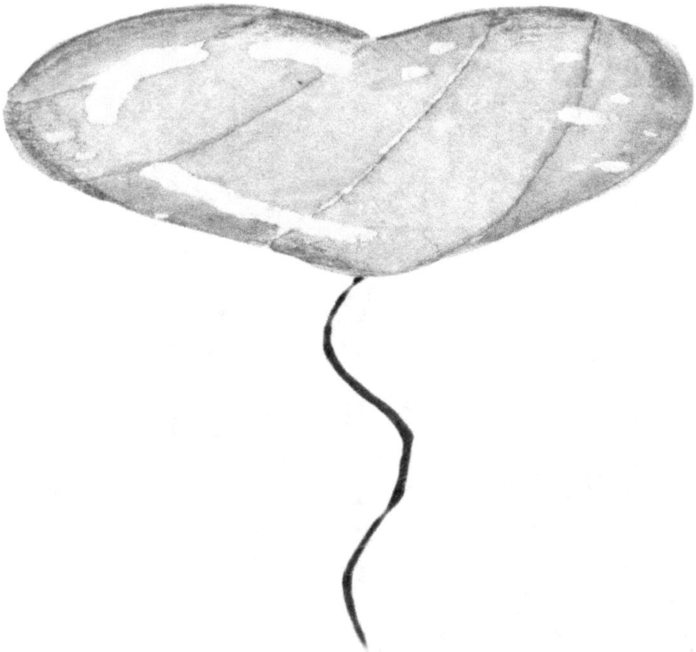

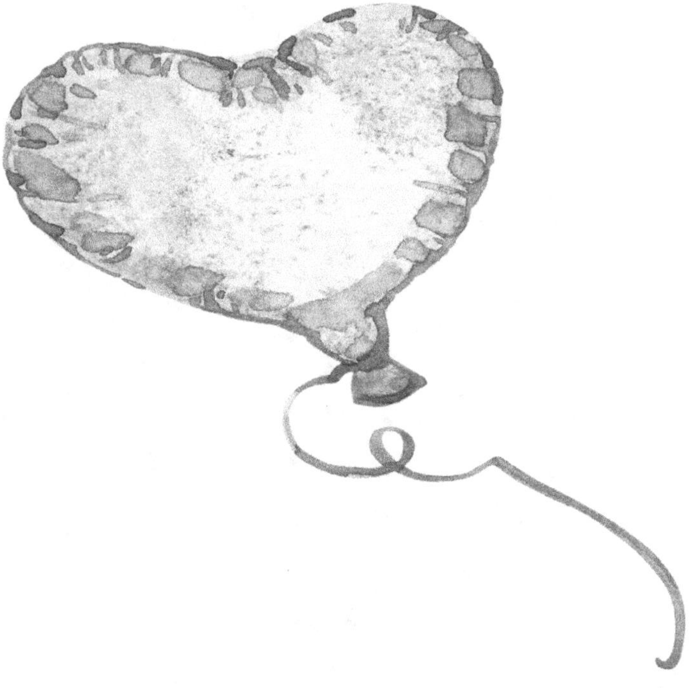

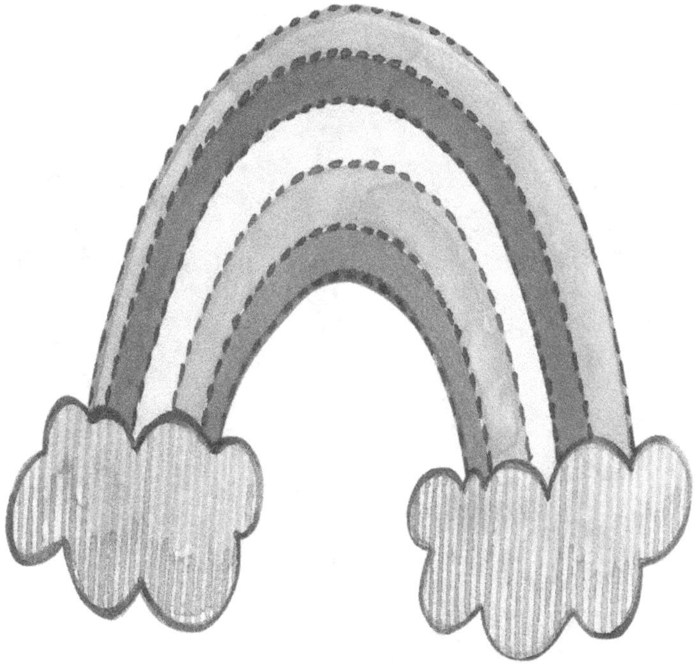

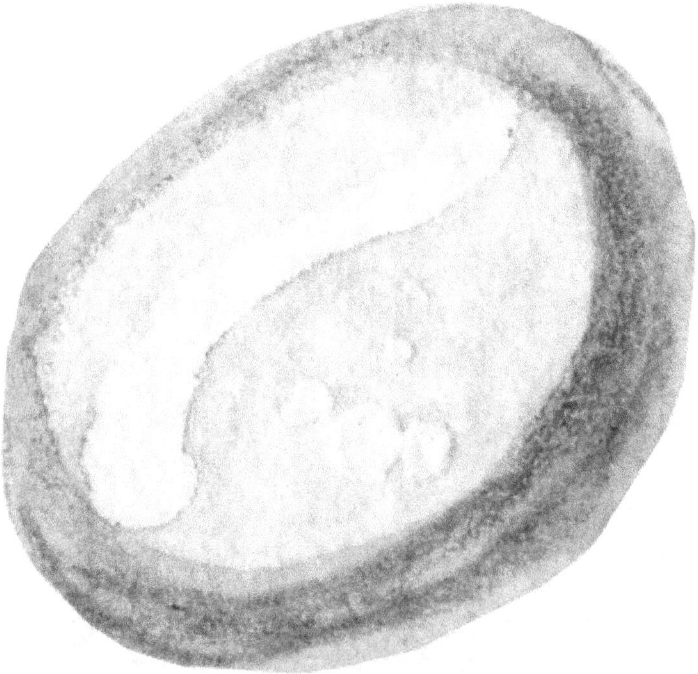

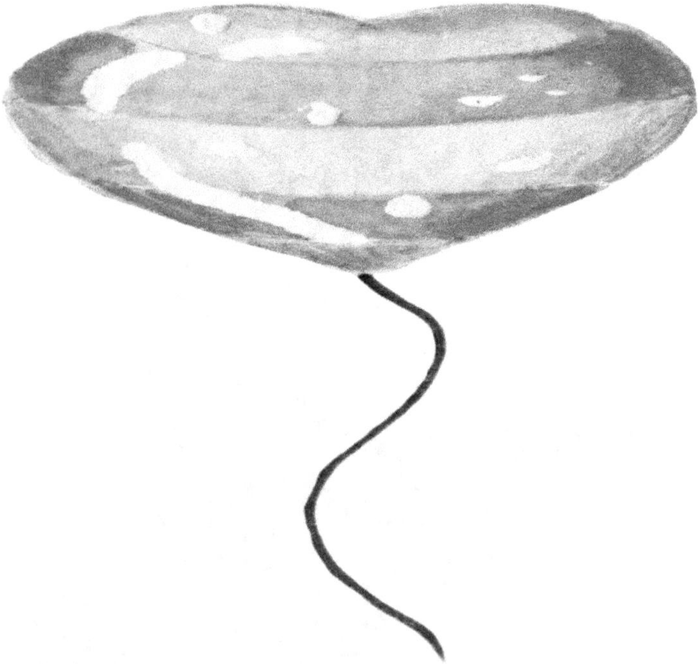

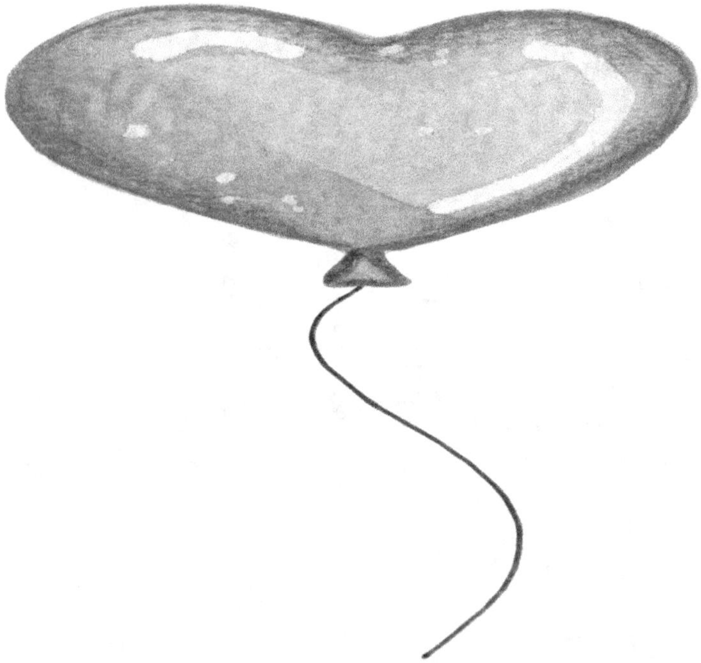

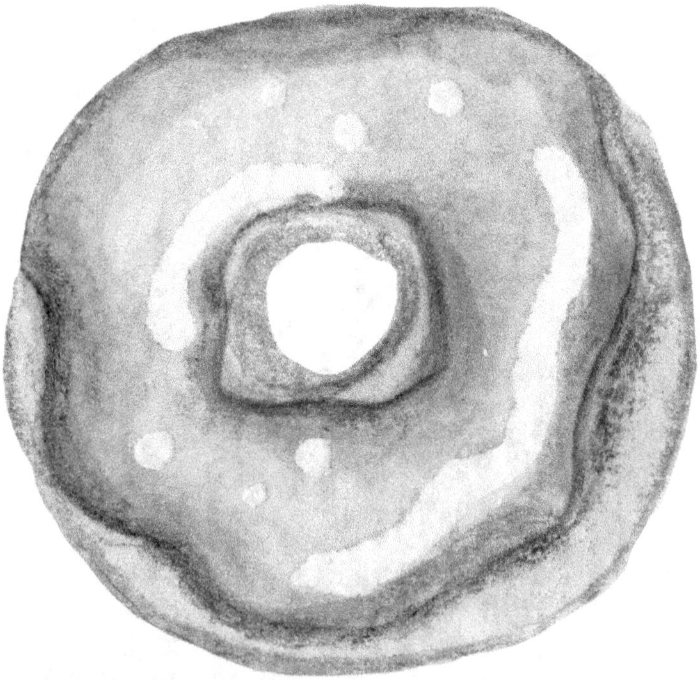

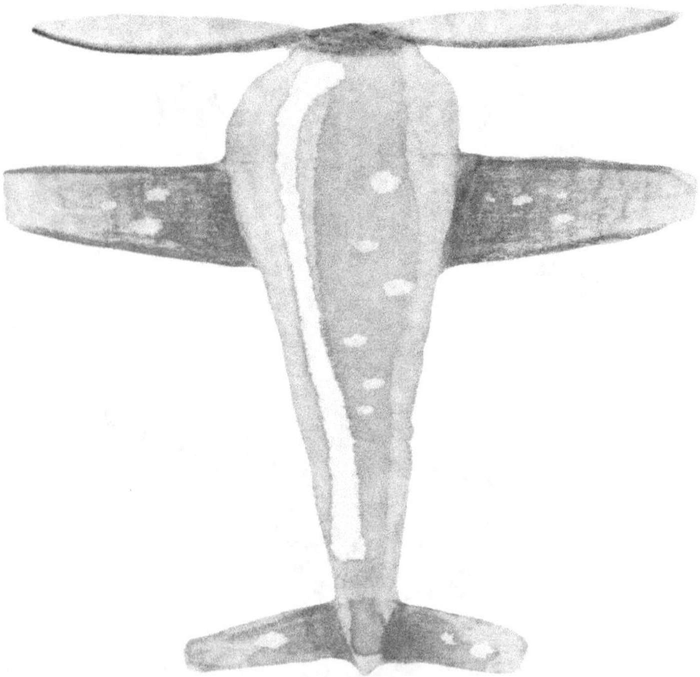

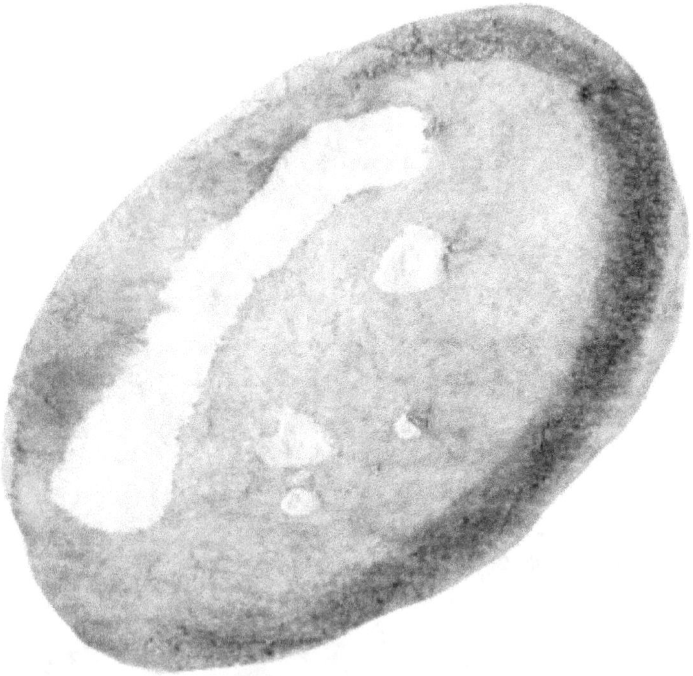

love

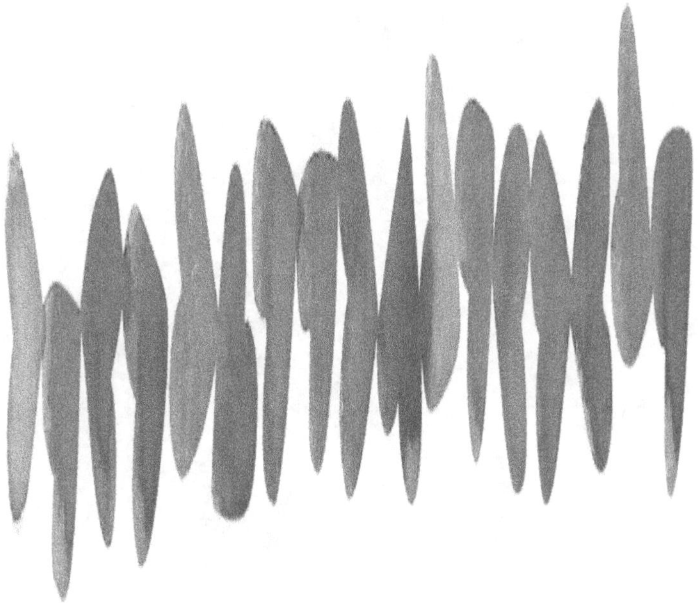

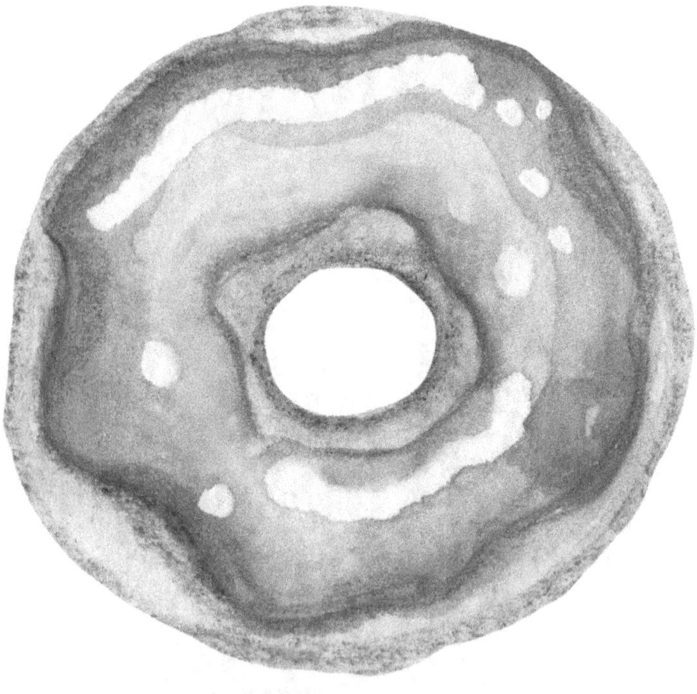

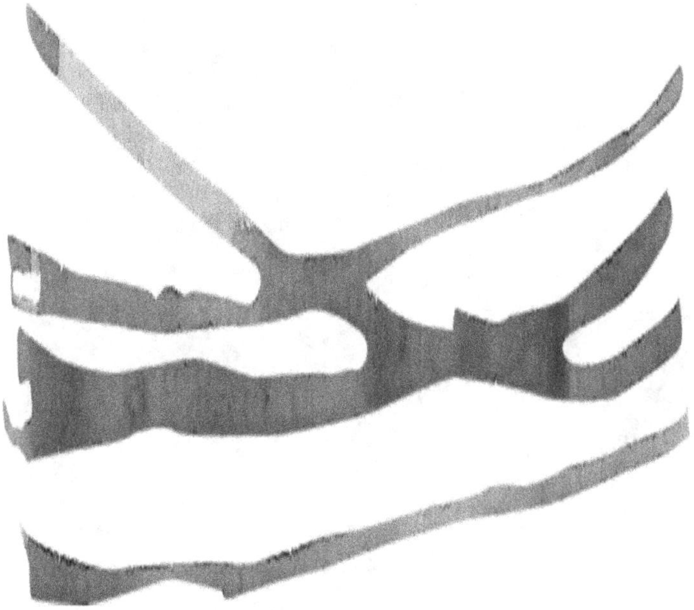

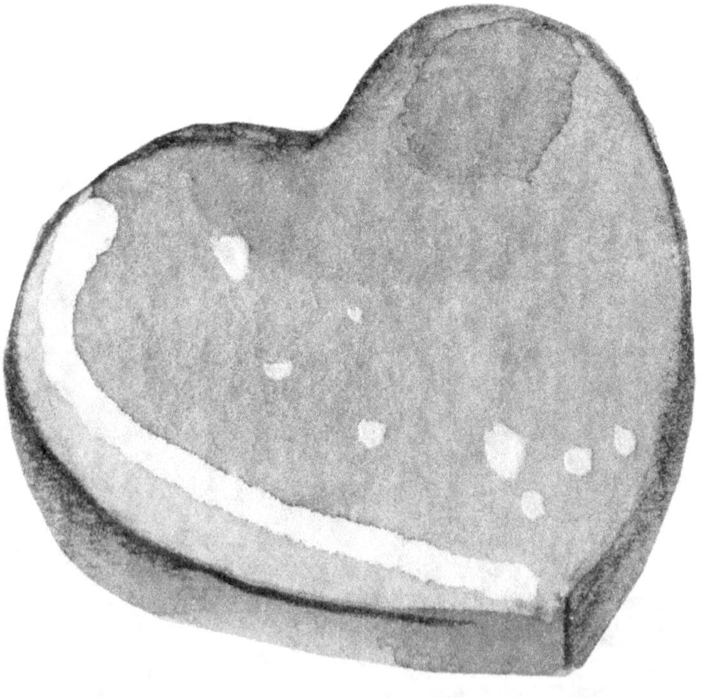

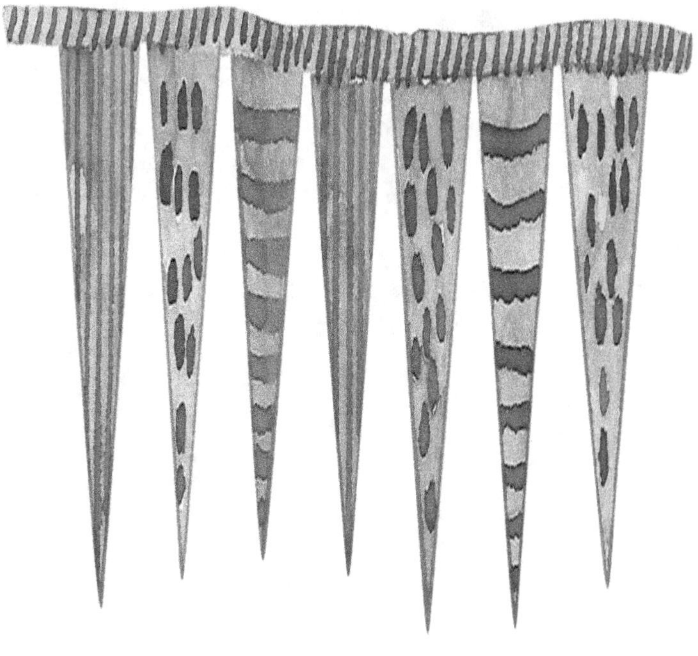

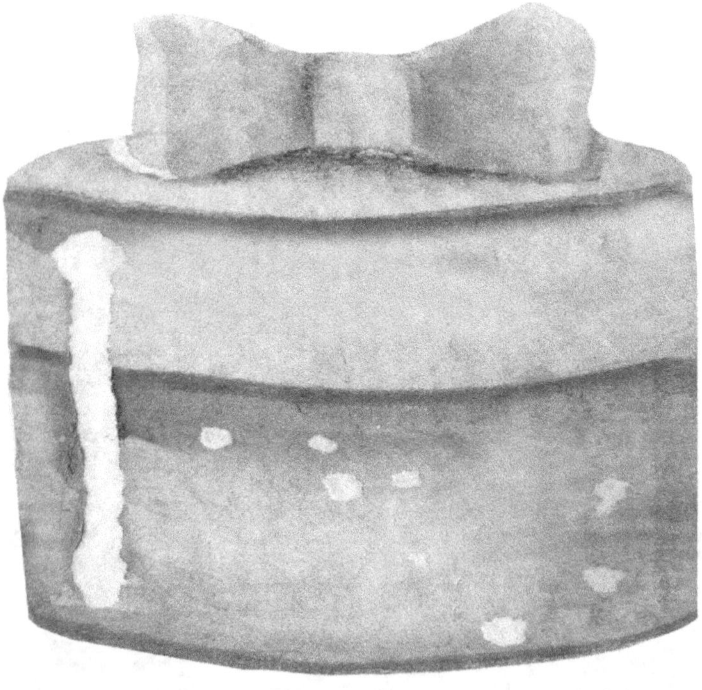

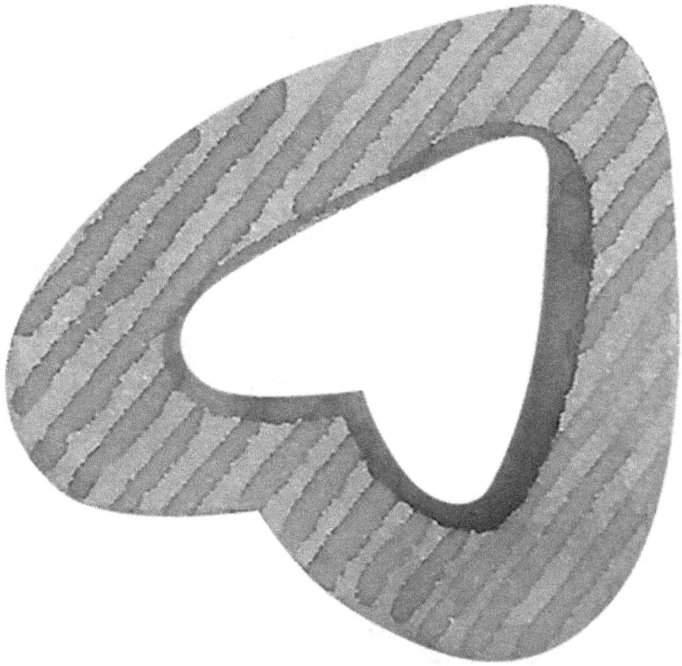

YAY

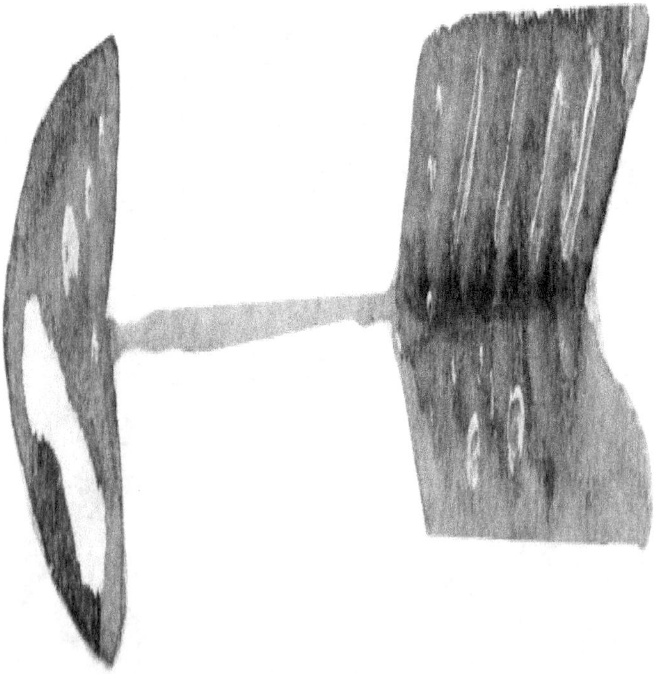

you
+
me
=
love

believe
IN
Love

love

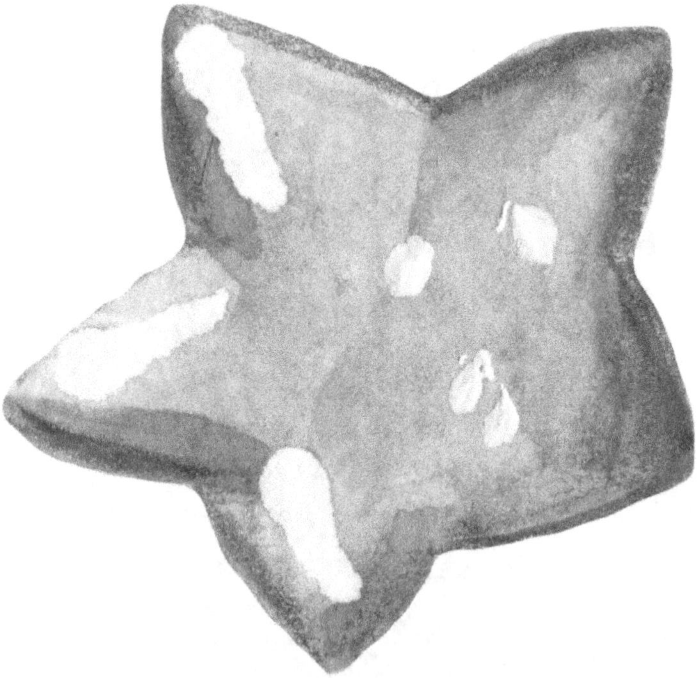

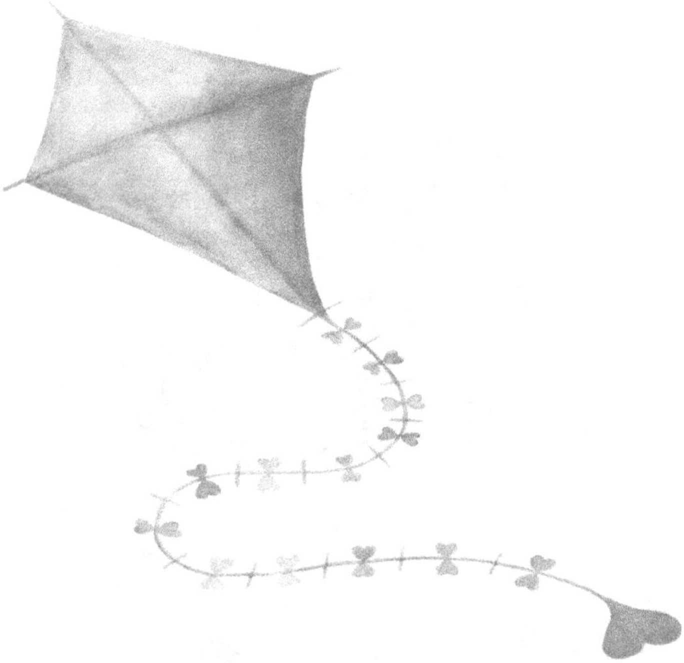

i love you

love you

Love

LO
VE

LOVE

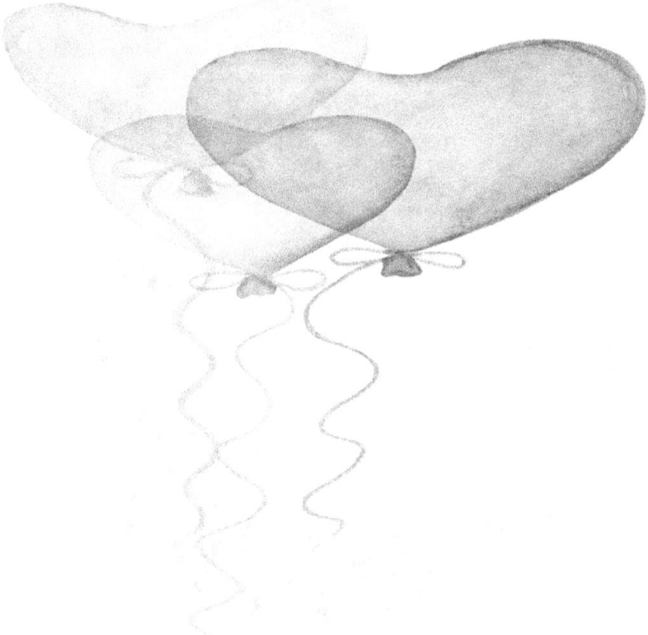

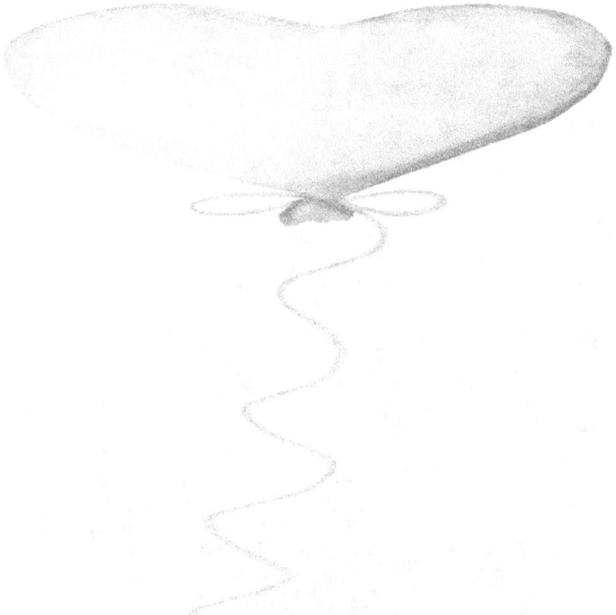

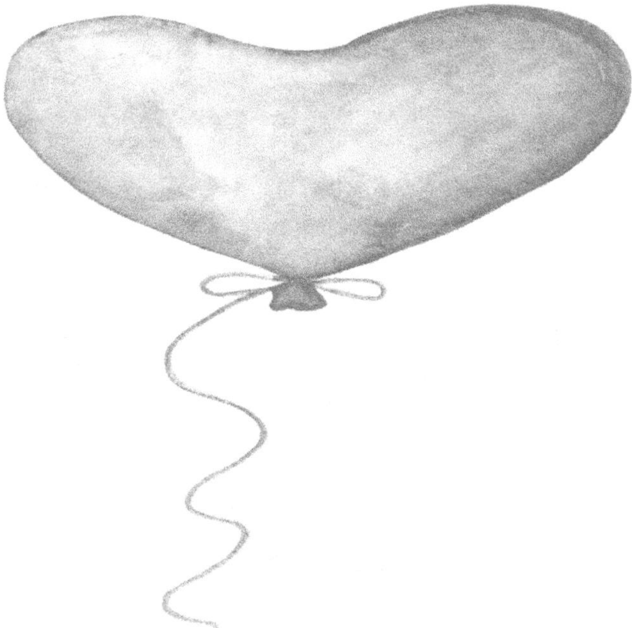

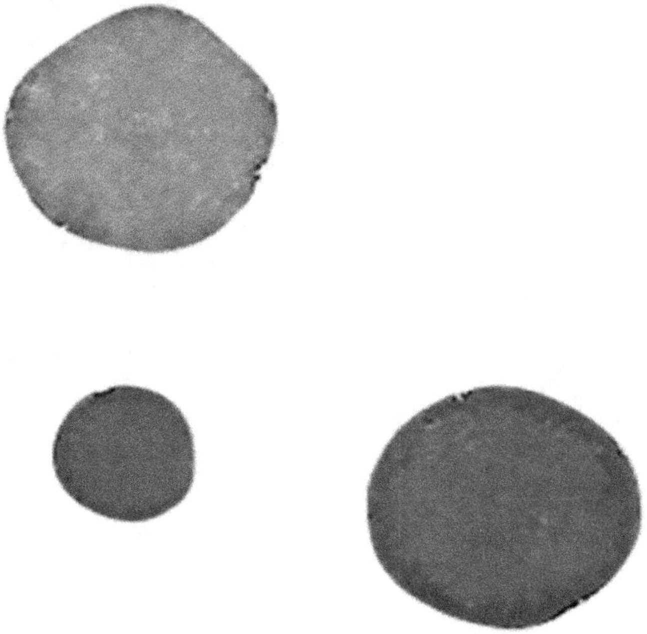

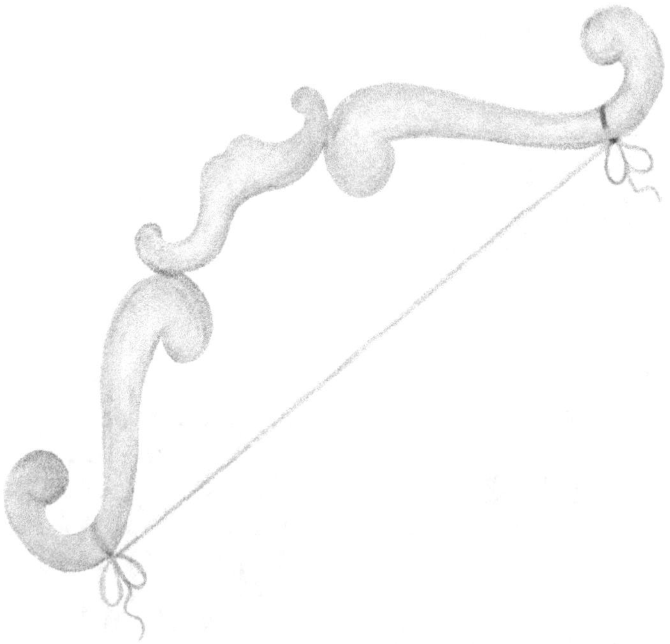

you
are
loved

love is all you need

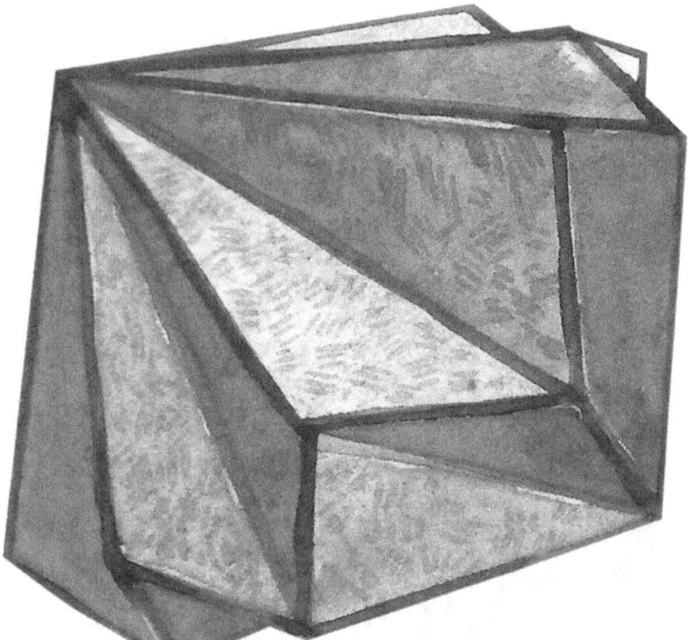

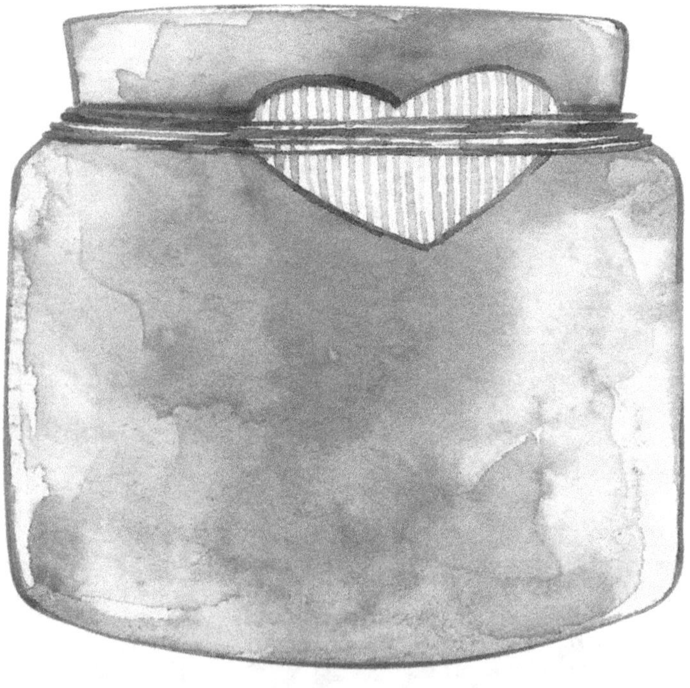

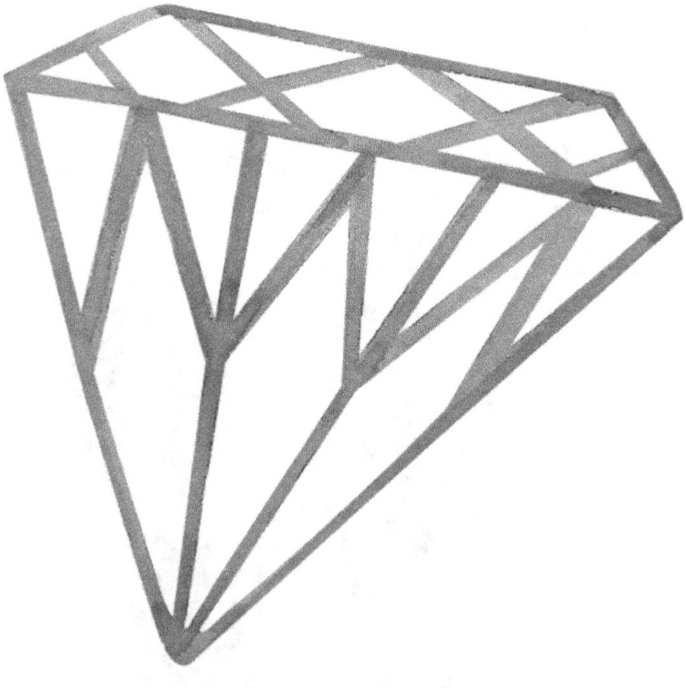

LOVE

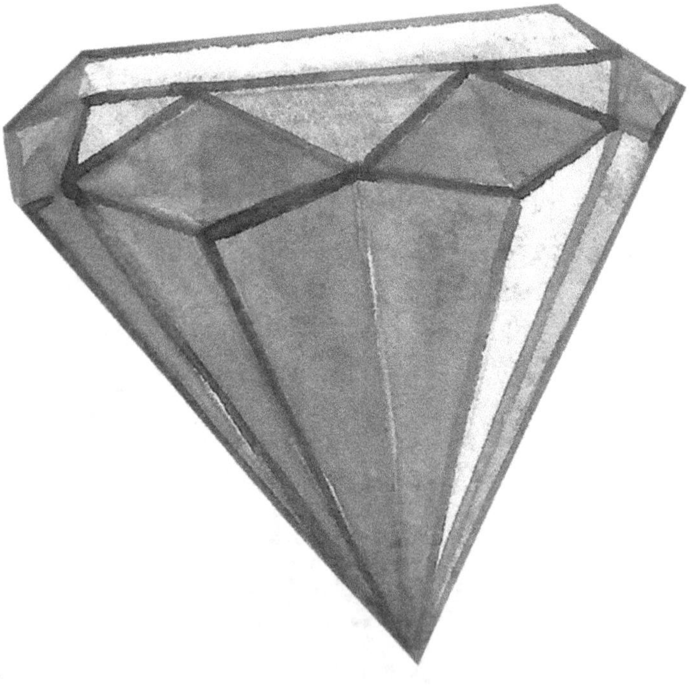

- Acts of Kindness Tracker -

- Acts of Kindness Tracker -

- Acts of Kindness Tracker -

Notes

Notes

Notes

www.ingramcontent.com/pod-product-compliance
Lightning Source LLC
LaVergne TN
LVHW060138080526
838202LV00049B/4021

* 9 7 8 3 3 4 7 0 3 2 3 8 5 *